Fun STEM Challenges

# BUILDING BOATS THAT FLOAT

by Marne Ventura

PEBBLE
a capstone imprint

Pebble Plus is published by Pebble, an imprint of Capstone.
1710 Roe Crest Drive, North Mankato, Minnesota 56003
www.capstonepub.com

**Library of Congress Cataloging-in-Publication Data is available on
the Library of Congress website.**
ISBN: 978-1-9771-1297-2 (library binding)
ISBN: 978-1-9771-1777-9 (paperback)
ISBN: 978-1-9771-1303-0 (ebook pdf)

Summary: Describes why boats are useful, how they float, and how to make and test a boat
made from foil.

**Image Credits**
Photographs by Capstone: Karon Dubke;
Marcy Morin and Sarah Schuette, project production;
Heidi Thompson, art director

Shutterstock: De Visu, 5, Evren Kalinbacak, 7, Michael Sean O'Leary, 1

All the rest of the images are credited to: Capstone Studio/Karon Dubke

**Editorial Credits**
Erika L. Shores, editor; Juliette Peters, designer;
Eric Gohl, media researcher;
Laura Manthe, production specialist

All internet sites appearing in back matter were available and accurate when this book
was sent to press.

Capstone thanks Darsa Donelan, Ph.D., assistant professor of physics, Gustavus Adolphus College,
St. Peter, MN, for her expertise in reviewing this book.

Printed in China.
2493

# Table of Contents

# What Is a Boat?

Boats float on water in lakes, rivers, and seas. Long ago, people learned to make boats to carry people and things.

# How Do Boats Float?

Why do heavy boats float

in water and small rocks sink?

Gravity pulls things down.

But water pushes them up.

Place a flat piece of foil in water.

Now fold the foil into a small piece.

What happens when you drop it

in the water? Which one floated?

Which one sank?

The flat foil rests on more water

than foil when it is folded.

It floats while the folded foil sinks.

The same thing happens with boats.

# Make Your Own

Now let's make a boat.

Grab squares of foil and pennies.

What else might you use?

Shape the foil into a boat.

Does it sink or float?

Water pushes up on a boat
to help it float. A boat that
is too heavy, or dense, sinks.

# Test It

Your boat floats now.

But can it go fast across the water?

Blow on it. What can you do

to make the boat go faster?

Boats need to carry things.
Add pennies to your boat one
at a time. What happens when
you stack them? Now spread them
out evenly. What has changed?

# What Did You Learn?

Boats float best when they are shaped like a bowl with a flat bottom. Spreading the pennies out evenly works better than stacking them in one spot.

# Glossary

**dense**—made up of parts that are close together

**float**—to rest on water without sinking

**gravity**—the downward pull of the earth

**sink**—to drop down into liquid

# Read More

Gaertner, Meg. *Make a Powered Boat.* Chicago: Norwood House Press, 2018.

Veitch, Catherine. *Big Machines Float!* Chicago: Heinemann Library, 2015.

Wilder, Nellie. *Staying Afloat.* Huntington Beach, CA: Teacher Created Materials, 2019.

# Internet Sites

*How Do Boats Float?*
https://wonderopolis.org/wonder/how-do-boats-float

*Why Do Boats Float?*
https://pbskids.org/designsquad/blog/why-do-boats-float/

# Critical Thinking Questions

1. How can you shape a boat to make it faster?

2. What shapes make a foil boat float well in water?

3. How can you test a boat for strength?

# Index